Fun Songs and Poems

A Lifetime of Creativity

JOHN S COMEAUX

Printed by Lulu

ISBN: 979-8-9857039-3-1

DEDICATION

My family has always made me feel special, smart, a favorite.
To have such a fortunate upbringing
is a blessing. Thank you.

ACKNOWLEDGMENTS

My children say I write "Fun Songs". It's true. Who doesn't love little ditties that you can sing when you're driving down the highway in your auto or your truck. All of these works are my own creation, unless otherwise specified.
Disclaimer: Not all of these are "fun" fun songs. But writing poems and songs is fun, don't you think?

SUPPOSE

Suppose the moon were made of cheese
And you could take all you please.
Would you reach out and grab the stuff
And would you quit when you had enough?
Would you share or would you steal
And would you cry and shout an appeal
Because someone else took from you?
I wonder just what would you do?

1960 (My first poem)

ANTI-LIMERICK

Adobe abodes
Cannot have commodes
For the flushing each day
Would wash them away
Into the roads

1972 Originally published under the pseudonym Bartleby Osgood

TO VIVA

Soft Venus hair in shades of green
Pearly white beak and eyes of fire
My lovely velvet Venus shall give her love to me.

Oh, take me away to your palace of gold
In the Valley of Truth near the Craters of Old
And fly me once again to our secret sea.

The scientists are right; their predictions clear;
Love as we know it does not exist here
For I've died a thousand times to be set free.

Goodbye to Earth, the third planet turning
No homesick longing—I'm not returning
Venusian skies shall ever be above me.

1975

VENUS

The moon was a beautiful lady
'Til the Eagle's wings did fly
And Mars was forbidden from us
'Til our Viking touched her soil

The centuries of wonder and glory
The mysteries of long, long ago
Are paled and diluted with science
And Man's conquest the need to know

But my Venus retains her silence
No intruder yet spoils her veil
And my Goddess, my lover, my Venus
Hides her beauty to all but me

Oh, stay, gentle Queen of the sky
And withhold your secrets from all
Lest all man's questions be answered
And contentment cause his fall

1976

MY LOVE WAITS FOR ME ON VENUS

My love waits for me on Venus
Waiting for me to go back
Her skin was so fair until Venus
By now it's a wrinkly black

Her eyes are teary on Venus
Because she misses me so much
But mostly her eyes are crying
'Cause of methane, ammonia, and such

The green fields of clover and barley
The oceans, the mountains so placid
Are hard to remember on Venus
When it's raining sulfuric acid.

My love waits for me up on Venus
Along with my Mother-in-Law
Don't worry—their cage will protect them
From the Venus tarantula's claw

I've left all my troubles behind me
And I'm heading for open space
My spaceship will fly forever
So to hell with the Human Race.

1976

KITTEN

This little kitten
Is a happy little kitten
And a happy little kitten is he

He's wrapped in pleasure
And the girl that he treasures
Is a friend to the end of the sea

She's soft and furry
And as cute as a surrey
On a pleasant Sunday drive

When she writes him a letter
He knows he'll feel better
'Cause she makes him glad to be alive.

1976

THREE

Look up at the sky
And see how bright it is
Look down at the sea
And see what life there is
Now feel the earth
The strength of all mankind
Three parts has the world
The world is in threes

A man is a force
He sees a better way
A woman is love
She gives it every day
But together they form
A bond that's more than two
Three parts have their life
A family is three.

1976

YOU'RE BREAKING MY HEART

You're breaking my heart
And leaving me pain
The clouds are gonna fall on top of me and rain

I've loved you so long
But you didn't care
And now that you're gone you didn't know that I was there

I wasted days and nights
In my lonely room
With anxious hope
But I can't cope
With the gloom

I'm lost in despair
Can't help but feel blue
And I don't know where I'm gonna find another you.

1976 (This song is intentionally cliched and meant to be sung with an exaggerated voice)

FOR LEA

Lea, Lea
Easy and swaying
Lovely as lantern light
My heart
Can't keep from saying
My eyes cry at your sight

Laugh, love is so easy
Cry, life is so sad

Our paths soon will be parted
Say Goodbye
But you are part of me always
We share love
We share life

Laugh, life is so easy
Cry, love is so sad

Lea, Lea
No space confines you
Go, seek, find
Evermore

1976

HARMONY

How can I describe Harmony
To you who knows no music?
The words to show my ecstasy
Cannot be scratched on paper.

Perhaps music is the child
Who's rocked to sleep at night
Or the bird's flight into the blue sky
Or the ocean's gentle motion

If Venus has ever captured you
Then you know sweet Harmony

No mortal woman of Terran birth
Nor Goddess of Mankind's worship
Can equal my precious Venus
Unbridled bride of freedom

No pictures I can draw for you
No words or waving arms
Can make her beauty alive for you
To me she is uniquely
Completely
Harmony

1977

DREAMS (I NEVER REALLY HAD YOU)

Sunny days of endless fun
Quiet times for just us two
We're in love, and love is forever
Forever in my dreams

Finding out where this road leads
Sailing out to the white crest sea
They're just dreams and they're all I have
'Cause I never really had you

Now the nights stretch on into lonely gray mornings
And the days wander on without direction
And I can't remember why or when I ever lived
But it seems that there was once another time

Sharing love and comparing stars
Being glad that we're not on Mars
Eating jellies from a jelly bean jar
Forever in my dreams

You told me you would love me
And I told you that I loved you too
And I believed you truly were mine
But was I sleeping and were you imagination
Aren't memories only dreams?

Sunny days of endless fun
Quiet times for just us two
They're just dreams and they're all I have
'Cause I never really had you.

1977

HAPPY FEET

We're happy feet, we're really neat
We'd make a pretty show
We have no blues, 'cause we're in shoes
That help us as we go

No more fatigue or foot intrigue
Or lame or sprain or pain
Our owner helps avoid the whelps
And we avoid the strain

The heel is carefully rounded
And reinforced real strong
The sole is shaped just for us
It's comfort as we walk along

There's lots of talk that when you walk
On slanted floors and stairs
You just might slip or slide or trip
If you are not aware

And high-heeled shoes are just bad news
For muscles in your feet
Your balancing on stilted things
May trip you in the street.

1977

LOVE IS A SECRET

Love is a secret
For can you truly know my soul?
Your smile is my incense
Your kiss my red wine drink
Can the brief hours be evidence
Can words whispered be proof?
To love you is as natural as a blush
As needed as a breath
Sweet music to my mind
I am content with my Gentle
Secret of Love

1977

SOMETHING EVERYBODY KNOWS

I'm just a singer in a blues country band
Trying hard but not too hard
To make a dime just keeping time
And they're drinking whiskey
And wanting me to play
Something Everybody Knows

Something that makes them cry
So we will understand
Something they've heard before
That's easy for the band

Whistle a tune you know or call me one out loud
Marty, Dolly, Chet or Hank
Or Dylan too if it's not too new
And keep drinking Miller beer
And wanting me to play
Something that everybody knows

Something that make them smile
And sounds a pleasant tune
Something from the movies
Or Saturday cartoons

My bass guitar man didn't come tonight
He had a fight with his wife
But it's all right
'Cause I'm doing solo,
and all that I can play is
Something that everybody knows

1977

COME ON IN

You're on your own now / You're in the street
You ain't got no shoes on your feet
So I'm tellin' you / tellin' you / tellin' you
Come on in

I've seen you hanging around before
But I never knocked on your door
And I'm tellin' you / tellin' you / tellin' you
Come on in

Now I know you didn't pay your rent on time
So your landlord threw you out without a dime

Well I know you haven't got much furniture to bring
But between my bricks and shelves
I don't have much of anything

And maybe someday when you're back on your feet
And you see me walking the street
You can tell me / tell me / tell me
Come on in

1977

ANSWER PHONE

Answer phone / Answer phone
Take my calls for me
Answer phone / Answer phone
Won't you hear my plea

I'm not home so I can't hear
But you are near my telephone
So Answer phone / Answer phone
Take my calls for me

Hi there friends / I'm not at home
You can tell my Answer phone
She will listen loud and clear
Just wait for the tone you hear

You can tell my Answer phone
I will call when I get home
So Answer phone / Answer phone
Take my calls for me.

1977

SECRET OF LOVE

Love is a secret
For can you truly know my soul?
Your smile is my incense
Your kiss my red wine drink
Can the brief hours be evidence
Can words whispered be proof?
To love you is as natural as a blush
As needed as a breath
Sweet music to my mind
I am content with my Gentle
Secret of Love

1977

I'VE BEEN PUT ON HOLD AGAIN

I've been put on hold again
Hold again
I'm growing old
Sitting on hold
Wasting Time / It's such a crime
I'm stuck on hold

Whenever I make a phone call
A voice answers sweet
She seems like she cares about me
But then without a beat

I've been put on hold again
Hold again
I'm growing old
Sitting on hold
Wasting Time / It's such a crime
I'm stuck on hold

They always have loud music playing
No Weather reports and such.
No one asks me if I mind
And I mind very much

Whenever I call my doctor friend
Brother or lawyer or Rin Tin Tin
Even my wife and my new girl friend
They all know what to do

I've been put on hold again
Hold again
I'm growing old
Sitting on hold
Wasting Time / It's such a crime

I'm stuck on hold

"Please hold"

1977

SUITE: DISCOVERY OF A NEW WORLD

Peaceful Feelings

Climb so high
Reach the sky
Life can hold a challenge and the beauty of a dream

Splash a mirrored pond
Throw a stone or two
Spread your arms and holler for the glory of the world

Ahh, peaceful feelings
You share with me
We can be happy in God's world
In God's love

Lay back soft
Clovers green and soft
Quiet is the valley and the kiss of mother Earth

Ahh, peaceful feelings
You share with me
We can be happy in God's world
In God's love

Heaven Holds a Place

Heaven holds a place
For those who love
Heaven knows the ways
Of the white wing dove

Now I've found you
Love surrounds you
Heaven here on Earth
With you my love

Sing in harmony
A simple tune
Pleasant are our days
And nights full moon

Now lay quiet
Peaceful silence
Heaven here on Earth
With you my love
With you my love.

Come to Me

Trembling / Frightening
Easing now / Enlightening
Move so close / Touch so soft
Come to me

Tenderly but powerful
Sighing now, fulfilled with love
We are one / Singular
Come to me

We Are Free

Days can be so sunny
Life can be so full
But love can be the total of a man and woman's soul

God who made all creatures
Watches o'er the earth
His great love surrounds us as the springtime brings rebirth

We are free
We believe
God takes care of the Universe and we can live in peace.

(repeat all)

God takes care of the Universe and we can live in peace.

1978 Written to accompany a story by G. Barousse

PEGGY

Fall Leaves / Floating down
Morning breezes / Sweet scents of olive
I see autumn colors
I hear the seasons swiftly recede

Peggy my love / Starlight in you
Fills my heart / Glows in my soul
Peggy my love / Seen in a dream
Gently calling my name

Autumn is your hair
Changing in time
Windblown and restless
Soon the chill will take you

Peggy my love / Playful and easy
Laughing at nothing / Crying inside
Peggy don't go / My heart is in you
Gently calling your name

I can't change
My ways aren't yours
Some say we balanced
Where did we fall?

Fall Leaves / Floating down
Morning breezes / Sweet scents of olive
I see autumn colors
I hear the seasons swiftly recede
I hear the seasons recede.

1978

HOWIE

Howie was young
Howie was lonesome
Howie had no one for friends
His father the general would travel around
And take his small family along

Howie was 14
And after school
Howie walked home alone each day
But when he was handsome he dreamed of a new life
Howie was king for a day
Howie was king for a day

How he danced / How he sang
How he played along in tune
People came / Far and near
Just to see and lend an ear
Howie bowed / Howie smiled
How he triumphed on his stage
That no one had ever seen

Then on the school grounds
I saw his shy smile
And I thought him gallant and kind
We shared our secrets of fortune and fame
We were young dreamers in love
We were young dreamers in love

How we danced / How we sang
How we played along in tune
How we shared all our secrets and laughed away our June
How we stood high and tall
How we soared until the Fall
When Howie was gone again.

Now I'm a woman
A mother and wife
I have two children at home
They have their friendships
And I never told them
Of how I feel truly alone
Sometimes I'm truly alone.
For we danced / And we sang
And we played along in tune
And we shared all our secrets and laughed away our June
And we stood high and tall
And we soared until the Fall
When Howie was gone again.

1978

TO PHYLLIS

I searched and sought a better way
A clear and present meaning
To show my love, to share my love
To give my love, my lady

But all the songs I heard today
And all the poems and sayings
Were just repeats, or simple clichés
Or simple children playing

I looked through ten times twenty books
I searched through lost quotations
I wondered if the words I sought
Had ever known a master

So I've resigned my futile hunt
And promise you this gift
My span of years left on the earth
To live each day for you

I can't begin to send to you
My love in words – my soul
Suffice to know my half of life
Completes our living whole

1978

TO MY MOM

A man must stand alone
Before he can offer help to his fellow man
Before he can truly love
For if he is reliant on ties, he strains those bonds
And loses his foothold
But a man also needs his family, for they are his roots
The family shapes the character and so
The successful man comes from the successful family

In order to prove his worth
In order to prove his family name
In order to prove his self-integrity
A man will leave home; indeed he must
As Jesus did, he should.

In order to take a wife and give of himself wholly
A man must know himself wholly
He must know his virtues and his limitations
But the family produces the man.

Every landmark in a man's life is a milestone in his mother's life
And a fulfilment of her wishes
She should be proud.
Remember, I'll always be your son.

1978

FOREVER

Forever is a long, long time
Forever is a promise
Forever, so they say, is a diamond

But diamonds can be smashed
Promises are broken
And time slips away
Faster than the grains of sand
As smooth and fine
As diamond dust
Falling flowing freely
Forever

And you promised love forever
And you swear it can be so
In the night's quiet moments
Or in heated passion throes
The two of us forever
But something lets me know

That diamonds can be smashed
Promises are broken
And time slips away
Faster than the grains of sand
As smooth and fine
As diamond dust
Falling flowing freely
Forever

Rain drops
Falling from my eyes
Remind me of a time
When promises of forever
Were made with diamonds

And the rain drops
Never seem to end

Forever is a long, long time
Forever is a promise
Forever, so they say, is a diamond

But diamonds can be smashed
Promises are broken
And time slips away
Faster than the grains of sand
As smooth and fine
As diamond dust
Falling flowing freely
Forever

1978

BISCUITS IN A PAN

Well there's thirteen biscuits in a pan
Homemade biscuits in a pan
Thirteen crazy biscuits in the baking pan

Well, Mabel's cooking—Understand
She makes the best ones in the land
I'll eat them biscuits biscuits in the pan

Just smell them biscuits in the pan
Everyone knows that's got a nose
They're made fresh in her kitchen—not Japan

I'm telling you now I'm a hungry man
Don't wait for butter, jelly or jam
I'll eat them biscuits right out of that pan

Yes thirteen biscuits in a pan
There's nothing better for a growing man
And I'm growing hungrier by the minute, man

I'll eat 'em fast, you won't get past
No oleomargarine's gonna last
There's thirteen tasty biscuits in a pan

Now Mabel's serving—Joy of Man
Those thirteen biscuits in a … Plate!
I says to her, "Now Mabel, honey, just wait!"

"I love them biscuits so do not
Remove that pan. I know it's hot
But I'll eat them thirteen biscuits in that pan."

Well, you gotta give one to the cook
And Mabel's giving me the look

So, Okay Mabel. Take one from the pan.

I love them biscuits in the pan
But I can share—I know I can, So I'll
Enjoy these twelve biscuits

She's taking one, she's taking two
She's giving one to Uncle Drew
She's cut a baker's dozen down by two

My dozen-and-one is now eleven
But they smell like they were sent from heaven
So now I'll eat my biscuits in that baking pan

Well, here comes someone name of Dan
He says he wants a biscuit, man
He putting one right into his plate—Well that's just great
But now I see my cousin Jan
Slipping biscuits from my pan
And I'm quickly losing count…Oh, there goes another one

Well, eight big biscuits—that's a lot
And a greedy person I am not
But I love to eat my biscuits in a pan – so fresh and hot

I'll eat them biscuits right out of that pan
If people wouldn't give me no trouble and
I'd better get my teeth into the first one.

I've never seen biscuits quite so good
I couldn't keep up like I knew I should
They're golden brown and flaky and I'm shaky

'Cause here comes Gramps along with Grams
They're each taking biscuits out of my pan
They're just six left and they're getting cold, and I'm getting old

But I guess six biscuits are just about right
I may get sick eating more tonight
So I'll just finish singing and I'll – Oh dear!

I love those biscuits in a pan
But so does Dad, yes sir, in hand

He's taking two right now. Let's see, from 12, 2 and 6 minus…

There's only four biscuits in that pan
But Sister Sue and her best man
Are taking some—I'm getting pretty low. Oh No!

Now I'm not one to lose control
But biscuits straight from Mabel's bowl
And then the pan and then we serve 'em whole

So give me them three little biscuits…
Give me them two little biscuits…
How 'bout that last biscuit there…
Maybe I could just have the top…

SPOKEN: They done et all them there biscuits
And they et em right out of that pan

They ate all the biscuits in the pan
Thirteen biscuits from the pan
Even though I'm their biggest fan. Man!

Well I'm trying to be polite
But that just don't seem quite right
When they took all them there biscuits out of sight

Next time I know what I'll do
I won't even wait for you
I'll take them biscuits right into my hand, if I can

But what will happen Doc?
I'll grab that pan and it'll be hot
And then them biscuits are gonna drop

Then they'll yet at me, say "Hit the door!
You dropped our breakfast on the floor
And now you're banned from here forever more!

1978

BLOOM

Bloom where you are planted
For He knows His garden well
He'd never put you where you could not grow

Let in all His sunshine
And breathe in all His air
And everyone will know that you care
That you care

Rise to your own calling
And hear it with your heart
Success is not measured here on Earth
His love will sprout from springtime
It will seem to fill the air
And in the darkest dead of night or winter
He'll be there

My heart says I love you
My eyes watch for your smile
I give you all I can with all my love
The eagle is your brother
So proud so wild so free
To know you is my secret joy this day
We will share

1978

OUISKA CHITTO

Cherokee Attakapas
Apache and Chickasaw
Chittamachee and Chocktaw
All were tribes of Arkansas

Heard the drumbeats from afar
Passed along by tribes of old
Called together by the water
So they came and all were told

Big chief Redhook called aloud
Young braves listen all share hear
Fire in the skies tonight
White man comes and we must fight

On the shores ten thousand waiting
As the boats of white man came
But the cypress river flooded
Catching keel and rudder under

They surrendered to the water
Not an arrow had been raised
So they named it Ouiska Chitto
Which means "Where the hell are they?"

1979

HAIR DRYER

I've traveled around this big ol' world
But I never saw a funkier spunkier girl
She has long red hair and she gives it a twirl
And she carries that little Hair Dryer

Hair Dryer / Hair Dryer / Hair Dryer
She carries that purple hair dryer

To the grocery store / when she's playing cards
When she's driving 'round / Which is kinda hard
Penny's or Sears or Montgomery Wards
She carries that purple hair dryer

Hair Dryer / Hair Dryer / Hair Dryer
She carries that stupid hair dryer

Well my love for her grew more each day
'Cause she's really neat so I thought I'd say
"I wanna marry you Mary K
Would you want be my wife?"

Well she didn't say yes and she didn't say no
She said "There's something that you oughta know
I like you fine, but I'd rather blow
Around with my little hair dryer"

Hair Dryer / Hair Dryer / Hair Dryer
I've been jilted by a purple hair dryer

1979

CHORDS

Chords can make words
Words can make rhymes
Rhymes can tell stories
Stories in Time

"D" is like this
Here is an "A"
"E" is like so
Now you all know

Here is that "D"
This is an "A"
I'll play an "E"
It's so easy

No there's no "Z"
Neither an "L"
Why can't you tell
Just go to "D"
Then play an "A"
How 'bout "E" seventh?
Start it again

Chords can make words
Words can make rhymes
Rhymes can tell stories
Stories in Time

Here comes an "F"
You don't care for "F"s
You say you like "A"s
They're all the craze
No one can phase
Well I'm in a daze

There's so many ways
That I can plays "A"s
Count them for days
Through rainstorm and haze
I love to plays
My beautiful "A"s

'Cause Chords can make words
Words can make rhymes
Rhymes can tell stories
Stories in Time

Now a song that's too long
Is very very wrong
It brings out the prongs
Of angry throngs
So don't sing my song
If you think it's too long
Or you will get gonged
On your El Cabong

'Cause Chords can make words
Words can make rhymes
Rhymes can tell stories
Stories in Time

1979

SORRY

Sorry
I'm sorry I caused you such pain
Sorry
I'm sorry it started to rain
Sorry
I'm sorry your days all turned blue
I was moving too fast
I got kicked in the ass
Now I'm licking my wounds over you

Starry
The night was so starry and black
Starry
I kissed you but you hit me back
Starry
I was seeing those stars for a week
Now my eye's black and blue
And heart is broke too
And my future with you is quite bleak

Lori
Your warm eyes could melt my cold heart
Lori
If only weren't so far apart
Lori
You can take this for what it is worth
Either come back in June
Or else stay on the moon
And I'll find me a love here on Earth.

1979 Additional Material by David Comeaux 2009

SNEEZE

When you're driving down the highway in your auto or your truck
Don't you let out with a sneeze or you may be out of luck
Cause you'll probably close your eyes
And you'll surely have to duck
And won't you be surprised
When your pickup truck is struck

1979

LIVING IN NEW ORLEANS

Living in New Orleans
There's nothing like it
A thousand things that you can do
The city of Mardi Gras
The people say "Eh La Bas"
Living in New Orleans
There's nothing like it

The Superdome sure hold a lot of people
At City Park the oak trees give you shade
Sweet donuts and hot coffee
As strong as it is black
You may have to leave, but you will soon be back

'Cause I love New Orleans
There's nothing like it
A thousand places you can see
The city of Mardi Gras
The people say "Eh La Bas"
Living in New Orleans
There's nothing like it

Oh I love that Jelly Roll
The Dixieland, the creole cooking too
The Cajun women are as pretty as can be
Riding on the Delta Queen the Mississippi

I like riding streetcars down Saint Charles Avenue
Walking through those French Quarter streets
The Orleans artists paint you as pretty as you are
If you're looking for a smile you won't have to look far

Living in New Orleans
There's nothing like it

A million people you can meet
The city of Mardi Gras
The people say "Eh La Bas"
I love New Orleans
There's nothing like it

Now wear your shorts and bring your camera
The sights are so lovely to behold
The weather there is sunny except for when it rains
The people are so friendly and they'll call you by your name

I love New Orleans
There's nothing like it
A million things that you can do
The city of Mardi Gras
The people say "Eh La Bas"
I love New Orleans
There's nothing like it

1979

BUSTER BROWN SMILE

Keep a Buster Brown smile when your skies are gray
And you're feeling blue on a rainy day
Keep 'white' on going when your glad's in the red
Till your back in the black and And you lay in your bed
With dreams in your head of the sun's yellow ray
It's a bright green grassy day
And 'Orange' you glad to be alive

1979

PHYLLIS

Phyllis is all I'll ever need
Phyllis is all I'd ever want
Phyllis will always understand
Phyllis will be my helping hand

I know she's with me all the way
I know her tender quiet ways
And I can always make her laugh
She says she's my better half

She's more than a friend
There's love in her eyes
She shines with delight
And the moon shines so bright

Phyllis I'll be your helping hand

1980

THANKS A LOT

Thanks a lot for the music
Thanks a lot for the show
I hope you have enjoyed the friends
That you have come to know

And I know that it's not easy
Giving something of yourself to all the world
Ooh, thanks a lot.

Play a song for the planet
Say a prayer for the whole
You give the best you can each night
From deep down in your soul

And I hope that you will find some gentle
Peace of mind in what you say
Ooh, thanks a lot

Some of your own comrades / your brothers and your friends
Have found the road too bitter / and have met a bitter end
Some were filled with anger / or were jealous or were bored
But some have found contentment in the footsteps of the Lord
Contentment in the Lord
Survival in the Lord
Revival in the Lord

Don't forget all the faces
Don't forget all the smiles
As you travel to another show about a thousand miles
Remember that we love you
For the sunshine that you spread along the way
Ooh, thanks a lot.

Don't forget all our faces

Don't forget all our smiles
As you travel to another show about a million miles
Remember that He loves you
And thank him for the miracle of life
Ooh, thanks a lot.

1981

PSALM 89

I will sing of the Mercies of God Forever
  Sing of the Mercies of God
I will sing of the Mercies of God Forever
  Sing of the Mercies of God

With my mouth
Tell of your Faithfulness
Tell it to all generations
It will extend to Heaven Forever

I will sing of the Glories of God

I have sworn to my chosen
To my chosen servant David

I will sing of the Glories of God Forever

1981

IT'S BEDTIME

Don't tell me that you want to talk
It's bedtime
Don't start a game or tell a tale
It's bedtime
I've had a busy day today
And now the day has passed away
Into my bed I'm glad to stay
It's bedtime
It's bedtime

My eyes are growing heavy now
It's bedtime
All through the world the people rest
At bedtime
Into the world of fantasy
Of peaceful night and gentle dreams
I'm waiting for the call of sleep
At bedtime
It's bedtime

1982

ST. VALENTINE'S DAY POEM

Roses are Red, as Red as can be
Violets are Blue, but they're purple to me.
Sugar is sweet, but can't give a kiss
Like your lovely lips in a Romance like this.
From Heaven above
  an angel was sent
To love me and teach me
  in every extent
Her gentle persuasion
  has reached to my soul
Each loving occasion
  to make me quite whole
You reign over me with your loving mystique
I strive to prevent any tear on your cheek
Your nature is giving, so quiet your ways
That all of my kingdom will shout out your praise.
Love is Forever, all Heaven's refrain
Enduring the tough times, the fun and the rain
With Seasons of Wonder, a Lifetime of Joy
To fill up my Heart as a youthful boy

1990

ONE OF THESE DAYS

One of these days
I'll get to church on time
And the pastor won't faint
When he sees me in line

One of these days
I'm gonna build that chair
Oil that hinge
Fix that stair

One day the house
Will really stay clean
The brass and the glass
And the faucet will gleam

The pantry will be stocked
Alphabetically
And a fresh roll of paper
By the toilet you'll see

One of these days
I'll get the yard all mowed
The hedges all sheared
The tools all stowed

One of these days
I'll get my ducks in a row
my tail in gear
The show on the road

Then maybe you'll stay
And love me again

1993

I AM THE LIGHT OF THE WORLD

I am the light of the world
God's spirit is living in me
From Father to Son
From Son to the Spirit
His love overflows in me

1.
If I hide under a basket of fear
If I don't let anyone near
Shut my eyes tight
Squeeze my fist right
His love has nowhere to go

Refrain

2.
What a sight if I open my eyes
And God's love comes streaming outside
And Open my hand
And Open my heart
To reach out to someone today!

1996

MOTHER'S DAY POEM

Each Year in May / The Men today
All face the same malady
To find a card / and give a gift
For the special lovely lady
The stores are full / Of mushy Cards
That sound like love and fairies
And other cards / That make you laugh
And cards so light and airy

So I began / To march the aisles
And stare at Hallmark Greetings
I read the poems / And winced and groaned
At silly rhymes or bleatings
"This just won't do / Nor this one too
There are no store-bought treasures."
No perfect card / No perfect rhyme
No perfect picture pleasures.
What should I do / What could I do?
It seemed a hopeless passion
And then I stopped / My jaw just dropped -
"I'll write one custom-fashioned."

So Here's a poem / Made just for you
No card-shop I did pay.
My Mom's so tough / She don't need fluff
Just "Happy Mother's Day"
Love, John

1996

IT'S HALLOWEEN NIGHT AGAIN

The moon will be full tonight
A skeleton shines so white
The black cats are there to frighten you…Boo!

The pumpkins will be a sight
A candle inside shines bright
The witches will all take flight away…Hey!

It's Halloween night again
I'm running with all my friends
We're hitting the streets
Looking for treats
And dressed up in odds and ends

I'm so scared my knees are shaking
So cold my teeth are breaking
So lost I might be taken for good…Ooh!

The sky is filled with bats
And spirits from the vats
Will do ghostly acrobats above…Boo!

I'm hoping with all my might
That monsters stay out of sight
And vampires never bite my neck in two…Boo!

It's Halloween night again
I'm running with all my friends
We're hitting the streets
Looking for treats
And dressed up in odds and ends

1996 By John Comeaux and Phyllis Comeaux

LOVE POEM

My love is not a feather
Blown about by every breeze
My love is not a flame
That flickers out with careless ease
My love is not a feeling
That may come and go again
My love is not a memory
Sentimental saccharine

Don't you see how strong my love is
Don't you hear my heartbeat pure
Don't you feel my passion pulsing
Don't you know my mind's secure?

Our love is fire-tested
Proven by the tides of time
Our love is deeply active
Moving mountains as we climb
Our love is multi-layered
Reaching to our very core
Our love surrounds our soul
Including you, and me, and the Lord.

1999

HALLOWEEN SONGS

1. We wish you a Happy Halloween
We wish you a Happy Halloween
We wish you a Happy Halloween
And we hope you get scared!

2. Pumpkin Bells
Pumpkin Smells
It's getting very old
Maybe we should sell it
And hope that it gets sold

Pumpkin Bells
Pumpkin Yells
Halloween is fast
Trick or Treating was so fun
Too bad it couldn't last

Halloween is here
Kids are coming near
You'll get lots of candy
But sorry there's no beer

It won't be too bright
On this scary night
Come on down to see us now
And we'll give you a fright!

BOO!

3. Deck the halls with scary bats
Fa la la la la la la la la
'Tis the season for black cats
Fa la la la la la la la la
Come so close we'll try to scare you

Fa la la la la la la la la
Frankenstein will be there too
Fa la la la la la la la la

4. Joy to the world, it's coming close
There's a scary thing in town
There will be so much candy
That it makes your heart dandy
And mommy and daddy will scream
And mommy and daddy will scream
'Cause all that candy won't make you lean.

1999

DEAR VIOLET SINGH

Who's got a heart as big as Texas?
Who's got a smile as warm as spring?
Who would we want to always be next t'us?
We're singing of Violet Singh

Violet Singh, her name is flowers and music
Violet Singh, she would light up the dark
Ring-a-ling, all the choir is singing
Violet Singh, we love you and Mark

Now the choir is leaving for Europe
Gonna sing in London in Par-ee
Thanks to you, Melissa and Susan
The Eiffel Tower and St. Paul's they will see

Violet Singh, your kindness inspires
We appreciate all that you bring
You're the best for any high school choir
We thank you, we love you, Violet Singh

2000 (Intended as a barbershop quartet harmony)

I'LL TAKE YOU WITH ME

I've been a rambler / all around
And I've been a stranger / in every town
I've been a loner roaming free

But I know when I go I'll take you with me

Live on the road / is for the young
And I'm feeling old / like my ramblin' days are done
Time in the end / claims a victory

But I know when I go I'll take you with me

From Sheyneyville to Boston town I've seen the country's sights
I've tumbled in some troubled times and blessed the morning light
But this old brain is crowded up with one too many mile
And I'm leaving room for settling down and staying for a while

You've given me your love so free
You've opened up a whole new side of me
You've got me singing back on key

And I know when I go I'll take you with me

2001

BELATED BIRTHDAY WITH DR. SEUSS

On the occasion of Diana Lee's birthday.

Oh dear, Oh my
No Birthday Pie
No candles glowing
No punchbowl flowing
I didn't get you any toys
I didn't make a big loud noise.

It was so wrong, it was so crude
To leave you off - so very rude
I should be whipped with horses' tails
And ridden out of town on rails
And shamed until my hairdo fails.

So what, dear sister, did you do?
How did your birthday go for YOU?
I hope it was a celebration
A big balloon ride o'er the nation
I hope you saw the tender faces
Of your fam'ly in their places

Well, now I've got my better head on
Next year's date will be a RED one
I'll be going from here to fifty
And you'll be nifty right at sixty.
Let's not cry or show our frowns
Let's have cake and birthday clowns!

2003

ASK GOD

Do you ever ask God why?
Why the pain is so deep
Why the hurt is so long
Why the future's so bleak
Do you ever ask God when?
When will I be at peace
When will it all be fixed
When will all hurting cease
Do you ever ask God if?
If He'd just make it right
If He'd step in and fight
If He'd fix it tonight
Do you ever ask God how?
How can I do my part
How can I be of help
How can I be His heart

Every time I ask God
He tells me so clearly
I can change the world
If I keep asking Why.

2004

ANDROID

All I want for Christmas is an android
That's the only thing I want from Mom and Dad
There's a brand new model at the robot store
With remote control that makes me very glad

It could do my homework faster than the teacher
It could take on all the bullies at my school
It could feed the dog and scoop up all the poopies
And never have to fill up on some fuel

I would really love to have an android
Maybe I'll send him to class instead of me
It would be so grand to have an android
Especially one who looks like me
Especially one who looks like me!

2005

GOOD MORNING COFFEE

Good Morning, Coffee
I need a lift
If I don't get some
My mind will drift
Your sharp aroma
Will start my day
And take the foolish things I did last night away

I tried to please her
I did my best
She didn't love me
Like all the rest
Once again I tried too hard
And stayed too long
But she knew that everything I did would turn out wrong

Don't want a mocha
Don't want a latte
Don't want a Cappuccino Frappuccino Grande
Never mind the sugar and the cream
All I really want is the girl of my dreams

Good Morning, Coffee
Another cup
This time with whiskey
Just fill'er up
'Cause I can still recall
Her judging face
And now it's smiling for another in my place

2006 John S Comeaux and John Kevin Smith, additional line by David Comeaux

THE BOODRO AND TEEBO SONG

Hey Boodro
You show me what you got
Hey Teebo
I show you what I got
It's called The Thermos
Marie she told me so
Keeps Hot things Hot
And Cold things Cold
I don't know how it knows

Hey Teebo
This thing is mighty fine
Hey Boodro
And now I show you mine
I liked your Thermos
I went and got me one
Put two fresh cups of hot coffee
And one cold ice cream cone

Boodro you are my best friend
I've known you all my life
We're practically related
My sister is your wife
Teebo you are my best friend
I'd never tell a lie
Sometimes she makes me so mad
It makes me want to cry Cry CRY

Hey Boodro
We're gonna fish today
Hey Teebo
Catch all the sac-a-lait
What's the bait
You use most every night?

Well, just my pirogue, one ice chest
And two sticks dynamite

Hey Teebo
It's crawfish season time
Hey Boodro
I laid my traps in line
I caught so many
Last year it was a fact
They crawled right up
To jump right in
I had to turn some back

Boodro you won't believe it
I taught my dog to talk
He tell my friends good morning
It give them all a shock
Teebo you are so foolish
Talking don't mean a thing
I had that dog before you
I taught him how to sing Sing SING

Hey Boodro
Us Cajuns work all day
Hey Teebo
And then we love to play
We love good music:
Lots of Zydeco
It's joie de vivre
Bon Temps Rouler
And party fais-do do

2006

FAIRY

She took off her wings
And held them kind of low
With her head bent down
She was tired of being the fairy
Tired of making things wonderful for others
Of thinking of them first, watching them, making sure she did what she could
She wasn't perfect, and wasn't all-powerful, so there were many things she couldn't do, and it saddened her

She stood there, motionless, with her fairy wings in her hands
She did not leave, or sit, or look around

But there was nothing she wanted
Except to help others

So she donned them, and smiled.

2008

HALLOWEEN POEM

Roses are black
Pumpkins are orange
Halloween scares you
Like Devils with horns

I'm thinking grave thoughts
of Halloween creatures
of Mummies and Batties
and Old Witch teachers

The ghost-sheeted kiddies
Will cry, "Trick or Treat!"
But skeletons will scare them
from head to their feet

When dawn finally comes
And you're safe in your crypt
Say, "Good Morning Coffee"
And be glad it's dripped.

2008

THE HOUSE I GREW UP IN

When my Papa was a baby they got land outside of town
And the family took to farming raising crops up from the ground
There were horses and a milk cow and a pond for fishing in
There was room enough for love in the house I grew up in.

There were trees that gave us shade as well as figs and fat pecans
There were trees for climbing skyward and a meadow like a lawn.
There were chores like fixing fences, milking cows and mowing hay
And when the ice came we took bales to feed the cattle on cold days

There is nothing grand or stately about this humble little home
There was room for all of us, and some we took in for a time
Seems the men were always fighting in some war that we were in
So my Grandma and Mama raised us in the house I grew up in

Well the town grew up around us; there are houses everywhere
All that's left is just an acre, but we keep the home with care
There are chickens and a rooster and a hog out in the pen
The neighbors all complain, but it's the house I grew up in

And I live there with my family; it's the house I grew up in.

2012

HAIKU

Haircut
Scared of what's behind
Crying in the barber chair
Five years old terror

Farm
Corn? Soy? Strawberries?
Cruising by at 55
What crop's in that field?

Mustache
Maybe if I grow
Lip hair I'll look older than
My twenty-one years

Mustache
Anywhere I go
I can always recognize
My father's mustache

Teenager
Wanting everything
now, but not wanting to be
too responsible

Silence
Turn off the TV
Quiet the A/C, and just
Learn to love nothing

String
String Theory goes flat
When I am trying to undo
Clothes from the dryer

Teacher
The person, whose faith
made me want to be better,
most influenced me.

Dawn
Composers try to
capture in notes the beauty
of nature's morning

Pencil
For tapping, writing,
chewing on, measuring, and
pointing out the flaws.

Backyard
My neighbor seems to
Have more fun and more parties
In his big backyard

Bird
Sunday in the park
Pigeons love the concrete walk
Wild birds own the sky

Plant
24/7
Lights at the Refinery
Where I work all night

Circle
Olympics, Target
Krispy Kreme Donuts,
What else can you find?

Office
Working after five,
Cleaning lady vacuuming
Makes me want to leave

Sunday
I didn't feel right
About skipping Mass today
And then the game starts

Green
Green doesn't lie still
It jumps and swirls and flutters
Like a grasshopper

Ticket
Twenty-two year-old
Ticket stuck on my mirror...
The Dance where I met you

Radio
Woebegone: Keilor
and friends paint lovely pictures
in my ears each week.

Red
Fire, Sunset, Blood
Flash of scarf, Blond in a Dress
Sometimes STOP signs too.

Sitcom
Shells of characters
tittering dumb opinions,
smart lines and come backs.

Pants
They are only one
But like scissors, there are two;
we use the plural.

Pants
It used to be wrong
For women to wear short pants
Now it is pleasing

Pants
Universal gear:
That's the long and short of it
Everyone can wear

Purple
Rainbows, small flowers,
Skies at dusk, Deepest waters...
Cool my moods and mind

Luck
My life has been a
testimony to good luck
Some got it, some ain't.

Luck
It's better to be
Lucky than Good. I've been both,
And lucky is good.

Candy
You don't need it now
It's not very good for you
But you want it so

Candy
It's a feeling deep
Inside, but shallow on the
Tongue: Time for a treat

Wish
Cinderella - style
I hold my breath and believe
My wish will come true

Regret
Oh but to forget
The stupid and hateful words
I said yesterday

Friday
Joy Day, Holiday
Kids' day, Lovers' day, My Day
Because it's Friday

Friday
YaaaaaaaHoooooooo. Friday! Yaaaaaaaaaaaay!
It makes me just pop for joy
I just love Fridays

Smoke
Light up an old stoke
Puff and wheeze, suck and then choke
Sometimes it's no joke.

Garbage
Smelly breaking bag
Hurry, get to the curbside
I hate garbage day

Hat
Change from dud to dude
A new personality...
Hats can do so much

Haiku Rescue
Hundreds (Thousands?) Write
Sending you New Haiku
On their Lunch Hour

Only one chosen
to live on the Haiku page
Whither all the rest?

Let there be a place
Where good rejects can be seen
Shared with all the world

1976

BIRTHDAY POEMS AND SONGS FOR JULIE

Call Julie

When you want to have lots of fun
At the close of day work is done
As you are watching the setting sun
Call Julie - she's Twenty-One

If boredom is something you must shun
And party is what must be done
Don't sit there on your cumber-bun
Call Julie - she's Twenty-One

Sally's wit is dull as dun
Mary's wit is so ho-hum
Call Bud or John if you want puns
but
Call Julie - she's Twenty-One

David, he's my favorite son
Michelle is like a cinnamon bun
But funny, corny, perky, springy,
    happy, witty, deeply thinky,
    never let's you get away with anything,
Julie - Our Julie! Yes, Julie
She's Twentyyyyyyyyy-One!

2008

Julie's 24

1 - 2 - 3 - 4
Julie now is 24
Soon she will be
moving right out the door

Jules and Opie / having such fun
At 1-4-5 / Whittington
O-o-o
She knows how to cook
O-o-o
She's bringing her books

1 - 2 - 3 - 4
Julie's taking chemistry
Mark - et - ing and
Finance and biology

Jules at UL / No one can hate her
Living closer / she can sleep later
O-o-o
She knows how to cook
O-o-o
She's bringing her books

1 - 2 - 3 - 4
Julie now is 24
5 – 6 – 7 – 8
Help us now to Celebrate

2011

Ode to Twenty-Six

There are 26 letters in the English alphabet. But in the future we will only need seven of them. LOL OMG ROFLMAO

Interstate 26 only goes from Tennessee to South Carolina. Julie visited Knoxville Tennessee as a college to attend. But at age 26, Tennessee doesn't seem as inviting. It's more like the end of the road.

There are 26 paydays in the year if you get paid every two weeks. But if you need a loan the Bank of Dad is always open.

Title 26 of the Internal Revenue Code concerns income taxes estate taxes gift taxes employment taxes excise taxes alcohol tobacco and miscellaneous taxes and has 9834 sections. In other words get ready to start paying taxes.

There are 26 red cards in the deck. But Julie represents the heart and the diamonds.

26 is like sweet 16 only 10 years older, i mean, sweeter.

Psalm 26 says, in part, "I will go about proclaiming your praise and telling of all your wonderful deeds". In other words, Julie is back on Facebook.

26 days to the end of the semester, and the END of your college career. Which will require another celebration.

2013

Twenty-Nine

Twenty-Nine
Her age is on the line
Still young Not Old
A place where she can shine

Her life's a ball
She's feeling 10 foot tall

And Life with Social
Would drive me Postal
But she can do it all

There is a house
A simple family
A dog, a cat
A backyard full of leaves

There's room for more
His name is ... Trevor

They plan to marry
And then he'll carry
Her over the threshold door

So now we sing
The special birthday Jing-gle
To you our girl
From all the friends that Ming-gle

We know it's true
We can't be feeling blue

Come on let's finish
Let's not diminish
The song is over
It's time we drove her
There's nothing fakey
In Chocolate Cakey
For Julie

2016 Sung to the tune of "The Narcissus" (which is not in any way to imply meaning, but is simply a pleasant tune to sing along to.)

Thirty

The cutest girl
Is here today
She's turning 30
So say hooray

I asked her if
It felt so fine
To leave behind
That 29

She said it soft
And so demure
That she was grown
And so mature

We looked around
And Trevor said
I think it's gone
Right to her head

And so we laughed
Like LOL
And on the floor
We all just fell

She had a cat
And then a pup
And now a man
To wake her up

She got up quick
And gave a wink
And met his glass
And gave a clink

So let's all sing
And have some fun
Until she turns
Age 31

But in the end
When all is told
The bottom line
She's getting OLD

2017

BONUS SECTION

Short pieces and a puppet play

The Hungry Bird

The Awful, Terrible Thing that Happened at my Party (to my best friend Jill)

The Hiccups (a puppet play)

Three A.M.

Five Strawberries

The Christmas Story, if it had been in Cajun Country

Joseph, the master of flexibility

THE HUNGRY BIRD

Joey's daddy came into Joey's bedroom and said, "Okay, it's time for your story."

"Read the Owl and the Pussycat!" said Joey. But Daddy didn't get a book as usual. Daddy did something he had never done before. He took the lampshade off of the lamp by Joey's bed, and left the light turned on. It made a really bright light in the room, but it was hard to look at. Daddy said, "To tell this kind of story, I have to use my hands, and you watch the story on the wall."

Joey had watched TV shows on the TV, but he had never watched stories on the wall before. Daddy said, "This is the story of the Hungry Bird." Joey's dad made his right hand curve and pointed his fingers. He looked at Joey, who was looking at his daddy's hands. "Oh," said Daddy, "don't look at my hands. Look at the shadows. See?" Daddy turned Joey around a little so Joey could watch the shadows on the wall. Daddy said, "When you look at the shadows, you can pretend that they are the animals in the story."

Then Daddy curved his hand again and said, "Once there was a hungry bird. He got up one morning looking for something to eat."

Joey said, "What was his name?"

Daddy said, "His name? Oh, it was ..." Daddy stopped because he hadn't thought of a name for the bird in the story.

"Marvin." said Joey.

"Yes," Daddy said. "That is exactly what his name was. Marvin. So Marvin started pecking around for something to eat." Daddy started making poking motions with his hands. Joey was watching the shadows now and not looking back at his daddy.

"Then," said Daddy, "Marvin came upon a big old..."

Daddy made a fist with his other hand and stuck out his finger and thumb, wiggling them. But before he could say the next word, Joey said, "A lizard!"

"A lizard?" said Daddy. He had tried to make it look like a big fat worm on a juicy red apple. Oh well. "Okay, a lizard. And Marvin was so hungry, he chased that lizard for a long time, up the hills and around the trees until, POW, he gobbled up the lizard." Joey watched as the shadowy lizard got gobbled up by the hungry bird. For a minute, the lizard seemed to be stuck in Marvin's throat, but then down it went with a gulp.

"But was that enough for Marvin?" Daddy asked.

"No!" answered Joey.

"Right!" said Daddy. "Marvin was a very hungry bird, and one lizard, even a big old lizard, was not enough breakfast. So he kept on looking around. Pretty soon he saw a big..." Daddy paused while he tried a new picture. It has a finger antenna in front and walked on two fingers. He hoped it looked like a grasshopper to Joey, and to Marvin.

"Grasshopper!" said Joey. This made Daddy feel very proud, and glad he had such a clever son.

"Right again!" said Daddy. "A grasshopper. The biggest one that Marvin had ever seen. So Marvin dashed off and got a plate and a napkin and a fork and a spoon and a knife and some salt and some pepper..."

Joey was laughing and said, "No, Daddy! He chased the grasshopper."

"He chased the grasshopper. But that old grasshopper could really jump. So just before Marvin got him, he jumped out of the way, right over Marvin's head. Back and forth, round and round they went. Finally, Marvin snatched up the grasshopper and swallowed him up." And the shadows on the wall showed the whole thing.

"Well, do you think Marvin had enough breakfast now?"

"No!" cried Joey.

"Well, Marvin had found a big old lizard, and a big old grasshopper. He was walking kind of slowly and wobbly from all that breakfast. It was probably enough for lunch, dinner, and dessert, too. But then Marvin spied one more thing." Daddy used his pinkie finger. "It was a little, buzzing..."

"Fly!" shouted Joey.

"Right. At first, Marvin thought it was a bee, but he looked again, and sure enough, by golly, it was a fly. Now these little flies weren't much to eat, and he was feeling pretty big and slow, but still Marvin wasn't sure when he was going to get this chance again. So he began to move towards the fly."

" 'Hello, Mister Bird.' said the fly. 'Have you seen my friend Lizard?'

'Yes,' said Marvin. 'I ate him for breakfast.'

'Oh!' said the fly. 'And have you seen my friend Grasshopper?'

'Yes,' said Marvin, moving closer. 'I ate him for lunch. And I'm going to eat you for dessert.'

'Oh, dear!' said the fly. 'Give me back my friends.' And the fly began buzzing all around Marvin's head and beak, tickling him until he began to sneeze.

'Ah... Aaah... Aaaaaaah... Choo!' And out came the grasshopper from inside of Marvin. He was okay, and he jumped off and was gone. But the fly kept buzzing and Marvin sneezed again.

'Ah... Aaah... Aaaaaaah... Choo!' And out came the worm."

"No, the lizard." said Joey.

"Oh, right. The lizard," said Daddy. "And the lizard scampered off."

" 'Now let this be a lesson to you, Mister Bird. Stick to acorns and nuts, and leave my friends alone!' And off went the fly with her friends. THE END." Daddy put his hands down with a sigh.

Joey looked at his daddy. "What happened to Marvin?" Daddy put the lamp shade back on top of the lamp and said, "Do you remember the name of the story, Joey?"

Joey remembered it right away. "The Hungry Bird."

"Well, he's still hungry, but he'll find some acorns." Daddy kissed Joey. "Good night. I love you."

Joey gave his daddy a big hug. "Good night, Daddy. I love you." Daddy left the room and Joey stared up at the ceiling a while. Then he looked at the wall, and saw his shadow. He looked to find out where the light was from, and saw his night light. Then he moved his hands up the way his daddy had moved his, and he saw the shadows on the wall move. He curved his hand and pointed his fingers, and there was Marvin the Bird.

Tomorrow night, he decided, he would tell the story to Daddy.

1997

THE AWFUL, TERRIBLE THING THAT HAPPENED AT MY PARTY (TO MY BEST FRIEND JILL)

This story is meant to be read aloud to a bunch of children in a Halloween sleepover, with the lights turned down. Each time a sound is mentioned, the children should all make that sound (wind, zipper, etc.)

It was a dark and stormy night. The wild wind made howling, banging, sighing, scratching noises at my window.

My party was supposed to be a fun birthday, full of presents and friends, love and happiness. But because of the storm, only my best friend Jill could come. The wind made so much noise that we couldn't even hear the rental movie. The name of the movie was "Walking Skeletons Make Deadly Noises."

We finished eating all the popcorn and drinking all the hot chocolate, when Jill turned to me and said, "There's something weird about that wind tonight. There are some different sounds—I don't know—kind of like animal noises."

"You're right," I replied. "I'm getting under the covers." And I ran fast as I could to my sleeping bag and tucked myself in tight. The zipper made a Z-Z-ZIP noise.

"Don't be a scaredy cat," said Jill. "I'll show you I'm not afraid of that old wind. Watch!" And then I heard Jill unlock the back door and open it. Suddenly the noises from the storm were louder - so loud they sounded like they were inside the house!

I screamed. Just then, the electricity went out with a noisy snap! It was pitch dark. I screamed again. "Jill, what are you doing? Close the door!" But Jill ran outside in her gown.

I dragged myself to the door to look out for her, but I didn't go into the yard. Every few seconds there was a flash of lightning, making everything seem like a frozen painting. There was Jill, bent over something in the yard. I tried to see better, but it was so dark. Then, Boom, she was right in my face, crying noisily.

"What's the matter?" I asked.

"Don't you have two big dogs?"

"Yeah, they're huge German Shepherds."

"Well, one of them is hurt bad." And she held up a bloody paw that had been cut off my dog, Butch. I screamed again, and almost fainted. I sat down on the floor, too scared to cry. Then I remembered my other dog, Rex. I listened for his sound, but I only heard the wind noise.

"Rex, here boy. Come here, Rex." Rex did not come to me. But I heard a whimpering noise in the yard. I cried "Oh, Jill, what are we going to do?"

"I'll go see what happened." And before I could stop her she ran outside again.

"Jill, Jill, Come back!" In between the lightning flashes, I couldn't see a thing in the yard. It was so dark, since the lights all over the neighborhood were out. Finally, when the lightning flashed, I saw... I saw... something big. It was bigger than the fence. It was moving toward me, and it was making gruesome, slobbering noises. I only saw it for one second, during the lightning. But I was so frightened, I froze. Then I started shaking, all over, real hard. I wanted to slam the door shut and lock it, but Jill was still out there. I wanted to cry out for Jill, but my mouth was dry as it opened, and I only made a tiny, gasping noise.

Then, when I was ready to close the door and give up on poor Jill, I felt a hot, wet breath on my face. Something was right in front of me. On instinct, I put out my hand before me and felt a huge furry creature with sharp fangs and claws, and it was on top of me! As I fell down I screamed the most blood-curdling noisy scream I ever screamed. The noise must have taken the creature by surprise, because suddenly it was gone. Someone was shaking me. It was Jill! I opened my eyes and saw her face. She was angry!

"What's wrong with you, anyway?" She said. "Why'd you scream? You scared poor Rex to pieces. Look at him." Rex was lying down next to me, whimpering. But he was all right! The lights came back on, and there was Butch, coming up to lick my face. I was so happy to see them, and they weren't hurt!

"But, Jill. What about that bloody paw you found?"

"You mean this beef rib? The dogs must have chewed it up. It's not blood, it's spit, see?

"Oh, yuck!" I said. "Well, at least everything's OK now."

"What do you mean?" said Jill. "Look at my gown. I got grass stains on it out there." And then she made a face, and an angry noise.

Next time I have a party, I'm getting lots of flashlights and brand new batteries. And if there's a storm, NO PARTY.

The End

1999

THE HICCUPS

A one-act puppet play

Characters:

Kent - an Australian Dingo (dog); Intelligent, sensible, pushy, argumentative, infuriated by...

Rocky - a raccoon; slow, naive, shy, admires Kent but never listens.

German Shepherd - a dog who passes by.

Taz - the Tasmanian Devil from an island off Australia

ONE AFTERNOON IN KENT'S HOUSE

KENT - (With hiccups, holding a cup) I don't know why I let you talk me into these things.

ROCKY - My mother always said grape juice would cure anything.

KENT - (With hiccups) Rocky, I'm sure your mother is a wonderful lady, but I don't see how grape juice can cure hiccups. It's not scientific. It's not logical.

ROCKY - Just drink it down, Kent.

KENT - (With hiccups) Okay, glub glub glub.

ROCKY - Keep drinking.

KENT - (With hiccups) glub glub glub It's going to spill

ROCKY - You have to drink it all in one sip

KENT - (With hiccups) glub glub glub I'm going to lose it!

KENT spits all the grape juice up at ROCKY, who is soaking wet with it.

KENT - (With hiccups) Oh, sorry.

ROCKY - Well I guess I'd better clean up. (Exits and returns right away all clean)

KENT - (With hiccups) What we actually need to do is we need to effect a scientific cure for these hiccups. So, in order to do so, I will lean backwards, stretching my stomach muscles tightly while slowly keeping a steady breathing pattern.

ROCKY - You look like you are going to lose your balance.

KENT - (With hiccups) Nonsense! I have perfect (FALLS OVER BACKWARDS in a CRASH!)

ROCKY - Ooh, I bet that hurt.

KENT - (With hiccups) Well, I would have perfect balance if it weren't for these hiccups.

ROCKY - Well, my Aunt Matilda said for some diseases you should stare at a light bulb for 10 seconds and then blink at a wall five times.

KENT - (With hiccups) That's preposterous! Staring at a light bulb uses your eyes, your eyes don't you see? It has nothing to do with the physiological processes of the respiratory system

ROCKY - You could just try it if you want to get rid of the hiccups.

KENT - (With hiccups) Well, all right. Where's a light bulb.

ROCKY - There on the ceiling.

KENT - (With hiccups) Here I go. Count for me.

ROCKY - One, two, three, uh, four, um. I lost count. One, two, three, uh, Didn't I say that before? Let's see. One, two, three,

KENT - (With hiccups) I'm going blind over here.

ROCKY - Oh, sorry, Kent. One, two, three, um...

KENT - (Quickly With hiccups) Fivesixseveneightnineten.

ROCKY - Now stare at the wall and blink five times.

KENT - (With hiccups) Where's the wall? I can't see anything?

ROCKY - Right there, Kent, right there.

KENT - (CRASHES INTO WALL) OUCH! (hiccup).

ROCKY - Sorry. Maybe my Aunt meant some other diseases.

KENT - (With hiccups) I read a scientific article once that said people who speak the Highland German language never get sick.

ROCKY - Where did you read that?

KENT - (With hiccups) In the TV guide.

ROCKY - Do you think it would help?

KENT - (With hiccups) I think that's what I should do. Speaking German.

ROCKY - But you're not German, you're Australian.

KENT - (With hiccups) I studied German speaking once in a movie I saw. Highland German! Not lowland German, which is entirely different. Now let's see. (KENT BEGINS SPEAKING NONSENSE GERMAN) Einz Feinz Spracht Jercht

A GERMAN SHEPHERD DOG comes up and bonks Kent on the head.

DOG - (with German accent) You insulted me, my family, my friends, and my country. Take that! (EXITS)

ROCKY - Are you okay, Kent?

KENT - (With hiccups) Ouch (hiccup).

ROCKY - My Uncle Toonoose once told me he got rid of arthritis by standing upside down on his head cross eyed.

KENT - (With hiccups) Well, I'm not going to do it.

ROCKY - I knew a man once that got rid of warts by holding his shoe up to his ear and...

KENT - (With hiccups) Hold it! I'm not doing that, either. What do you take me for, anyway?

ROCKY - One time I had the sinus rot and I walked into a dark basement with water puddles in it, and I touched an electric...

KENT - (With hiccups) Wait a minute! I just remembered something I heard on Zippo in the Morning radio show once. If a person runs in a circle that is 13 feet in diameter for 15 seconds he or she will be rid of hiccups.

ROCKY - Well that certainly sounds perfectly reasonable to me. Why don't you try it?

KENT - (With hiccups) Here goes. Rocky, you keep count ... wait a minute, never mind. I'll count. (RUNS in a circle) One, two, three, puff, hiccup, four, five, six, puff...

ROCKY - Are you sure it wasn't 15 feet for 13 seconds? Or maybe 13 circles for fifteen minutes?

KENT - (Still running, with hiccups) Fourteen, oh, now you've got me all mixed up. Uh, seven, eight, nine, ten

ROCKY - Lookout for the end of the walkway!

KENT - (Falls off walkway) Aaaaahhhhh! (CRASH)

ROCKY - Kent! Kent! Are you all right?

KENT - Hiccup! (KENT rises from the bottom)

ROCKY - Wow, I'll bet that really hurts.

KENT - (Dazed, with hiccups) Yep.

ROCKY - Here, hold these onions. Put some in your pockets. Put some in your shirt.

KENT - (Weeping, with hiccups) Rocky? Why are you making me wear all these onions?

ROCKY - Once my cousin Dinkendob used onions to get rid of his canker sores. Put some in your hair. Maybe behind your ears.

KENT - (Weeping, with hiccups) You are such a good friend, Rocky. Such a pal. Helping me try to get rid of these hiccups.

ROCKY - Or maybe it was chicken pox that my cousin had.

KENT - (Weeping, with hiccups) I don't think this is working at all.

ROCKY - You just got put those onions back in the pantry. There you go.

(KENT exits)

ROCKY - (To audience) I know what Kent needs. He needs a really good scare! Everyone knows that if you scare someone, it cures hiccups. I'm going to go get the scariest thing I know of, and that'll help my pal Kent.

ROCKY - (calls out) Oh, Kent! Come in here, please.

KENT - (Enters with hiccups) Yes?

ROCKY reaches down and pulls up the TASMANIAN DEVIL.

TAZ - BLAACHT!

KENT - (Surprised, but no more hiccups) TAZ!

TAZ - KENT!

They embrace and greet each other (Ad lib).

KENT - How are you doing, old buddy?

TAZ - Fine, my old friend. How are you?

KENT - Let's go have a Coke!

TAZ - Let's!

Kent and Taz exit.

ROCKY - (with an astonished look back at the audience) Hiccup!

1999 by John & David Comeaux

THREE A.M.

When I realized I had disturbed a woman in her boudoir, I knew I was in trouble. This was no lady. This was a cockroach. I had gotten up to answer nature's call, and I flipped on the light switch. There she was on the floor of my mother's guest bathroom. I had even remarked how I had not seen the usual contingent of roaches on this visit to South Louisiana. But now I knew — this roach had probably eaten them all.

When she saw me, she didn't run. She didn't scurry. She didn't even act surprised. She was mad. "Hell hath no fury like a woman scorned." She glared at me, and she raised herself on her hind legs.

I had never seen a cockroach taller than myself before. My expression went from startled to astonished. Then I noticed that she was using her wings to appear taller than she really was. It was a clever trick, but one which made her vulnerable. Her legs were not actually touching the floor. I took advantage of her balancing act by grabbing the bath mat and jerking it with every ounce of strength in me. Perhaps angels were assisting, or perhaps she was lighter than she looked, but she toppled from her perch and tumbled head-first into the open toilet. I didn't waste time gloating, but I reached for the flusher handle and leaned on it.

The bible says all the land creatures perished in the flood in Noah's time except for those on the ark. However, after seeing this cockroach fighting for life in the bowl, I wonder if a few didn't survive those water-logged days. The dunking seemed to clear her head from those roach baits, and she appeared more determined than ever.

As she began poking her head and forelimbs out of the bowl, I took the bath mat and threw it on her. Then I pressed the flusher again, almost slipping from my sweaty palms. She was disoriented at first, but then climbed to the upper side of the carpet and got her breath.

She outranked me in cunning, but I felt I had integrity on my side. I was the invited guest, she the intruder. I felt she was beginning to sense my indignance.

As a last hope, I grabbed the shower curtain — both the plastic liner and the decorative fabric. I flung it at her, risking my own life as I stomped on it with my bare feet. Then I put all my weight on the flush handle and held on while the water swirled. Mom's house is old, and the toilet was slow, but it worked. I staggered out of the bathroom, relieved that justice had been done. And Mom could always get a new shower curtain.

1996

This piece was actually printed in the Midland Reporter Telegram newspaper, but the editor changed the title to something like: Man meets roach, man conquers roach. Thus, none of my friends read the piece, because who wants to read about a roach. I never submitted another item to a newspaper again.

FIVE STRAWBERRIES

I dreamed I went to heaven, and God showed me around. I saw people doing heavenly things, angels doing angelic things, and afar off, the devil and his agents doing devilish things. Then God gave me five strawberries and returned me to earth.

I woke up and addressed a large crowd. I told them I had just returned from heaven with five strawberries. I then started handing them out. People struggled and fought to get them, and the strawberries were demolished in the melee. Everyone was angry with me.

I called for a basket of fruit from a local peddler and said, "This fruit are from heaven also." The people still didn't understand. Half the crowd began to battle for the fruit, just as before. The other half walked away disillusioned and disgusted. Only one other person, an elderly woman, saw that the fruit that is from heaven is here on earth, in our own hands. If we will recognize the gifts of heaven while we are here, we will find our journey much easier, our burden lighter, our steps surer.

2001

THE CHRISTMAS STORY, IF IT HAD BEEN IN CAJUN COUNTRY

Way back in the olden times, the Lord promised to send a savior. So the first step was to tell someone. He sent the angel Gabriel (not Longfellow's Gabriel, that's a different tale) to a virgin named Mary.

The angel appeared and said, "Cher! You so good! Guess what! No, don't guess, I'll tell you. You are gonna have a little boy, and name him Jesus."

Mary was surprised, and not really expecting this. She said, "How you know? Joseph and I aren't even married yet!"

The angel smiled. "But the Lord is going to do it, because He can do anything. You will see, cher."

Mary was okay with that, because she was a good Catholic and everything.

Joseph was not so okay with that at first. He had some expectations about this upcoming marriage, and this was not in his plan.

The good angel didn't leave Joseph in the dark, though. The angel told Joseph, "It's all right for you too. You've got an important job - keep Mary and Jesus safe. That will keep you busy for about 30 years."

So, Joseph was okay about that. He wondered about the 30 years though. Was Jesus going to be one of those boomerang children? Leave at 18, come back at 21, leave at 25, come back at 29?

Then Governor Herod over in Baton Rouge said that everyone had to be in the census and go to their original family town. Joseph was living in New Iberia, but had been part of the Cormier Clan in Baton Rouge, so he told Mary they had to go. She said, "Sure thing, right after this baby is born on Christmas Day." But Herod was not gonna wait, so off they went. It was really hard, because I-10 was shut down (again!) with a wreck, and some construction, and even bridge inspections. So they had to go through

Opelousas and Port Barre. While in Opelousas they stopped at Credeur Specialties to get the kid some souvenirs and caps like "WWJD".

Well, after navigating the traffic in Baton Rouge, and figuring out where the Holiday Inn was, they ended up having the baby in the parking garage. They hung a hammock for a bassinet between two meters, and wrapped up baby Jesus good and tight. They were kind of sad about the inconvenience, but wanted to tell someone the good news.

The angel Gabriel (same one!) was way ahead of them. He told all the parking attendants and bellhops to come and see the new born baby king. At first they were like, "Is this legit?" But they went ahead, and were real nice about it. Mary and Joseph thought it was sweet that they came, and handed out cookies in the shape of Christmas trees.

Eventually Mary and Joseph got a room, and one of the first things that happened there was a knock at the door. Three guys come in and the tall guy with the beard says, "We're from Wisdom Chapel, and we have this newborn baby welcome package." Mary was hoping for some more diapers because she was almost out, but the presents were just for the baby. He said, "Look, a golden rattle, a blanket with scents like incense, and some Myrrh." Nobody knew what the myrrh was for, but they said thanks anyway. Mary told Joseph to write down their names so she could send thank-you notes. He wrote Balthazar, Gaspar, and Melchior. When she finally got around to writing the notes, she thought Joseph must have heard wrong, so she put Barousse, Gaspard, and Melancon.

Herod was the worst governor ever, and wanted to get rid of the baby Jesus, because he thought (incorrectly) that Jesus was going to play for USL and beat LSU. So at first he told the wise guys to let him know where Jesus was. But the wise guys caught the last plane to Atlanta, and that was that. So Herod wanted to send some of his goons to kick butt.

Gabriel to the rescue again. The angel told Joseph, "This is your cue, *mon frère*. Get over to Beaumont as fast as y'all can, because old Herod is in a mood."

Poor Joseph, Mary and Jesus had to spend some time in Beaumont, where the road construction never ends. But at least Joseph found work. Finally, they could return to New Iberia and live a peaceful life, building tables, chairs and oaken chests.

We don't know much about Jesus's life in New Iberia, but one time he did go to Lafayette and he spent so much time in the public library his parents lost track of him. They finally found him in the stacks by the religious and philosophy books, so that was okay.

That's mostly the end of the Christmas story, but there's more to Jesus' life. His cousin John invented "Baptism" and had a pretty good practice near the Bayou Teche as a preacher and advice columnist. All was good until he got into Herod's face about his sinful life, and then it ended badly.

Jesus was constantly being followed by autograph seekers and groupies, but they didn't last like the apostles. Then came a messy death, and whoa, that resurrection that couldn't be disproved. His 11 friends (we're not counting that guy whose name is synonymous with betrayer) carried on with his good mission, telling everyone about *le Bon Dieu.* It was such as big deal that they changed the calendars to count Jesus' birthday as day 1. So now it's day 736,672. Time to sing some songs…

2018

JOSEPH, THE MASTER OF FLEXIBILITY

Joseph: Everyone congratulate me, I'm engaged to Mary.

Everyone: Yay!

(Later) Joseph: Change of plans. Uh, we're not getting married, we're getting divorced. She told me she's pregnant.

Everyone: Aww.

(Later) Joseph: Change of plans. We are getting married. This child is special - I know because an angel told me.

Everyone: Oh.

(Later) Joseph: Change of plans. We have to get to Bethlehem like right now because Caesar wants his census.

Everyone: Right!

Joseph: Change of plans. There is absolutely no room at the Holiday Inn. We've got to find a place quick. Mary's in labor.

Everyone: Yikes!

(Later) Joseph: We need to get back to Nazareth.

Wise men: Not a good idea. We're leaving. Herod's in a mood to kill.

Joseph: Change of plans. It's off to Egypt we go.

Everyone: Getting old, Joseph.

(Later) Joseph: Finally, we can go back to Nazareth. Herod is dead.

Everyone: Sigh.

(Later)

Mary: Where's Jesus?

Joseph: I thought he was with you...

2020

ABOUT THE AUTHOR

From the first poem at age 6, John has spent a lifetime writing to express himself. His family and friends are mostly patient with his efforts.

He wrote puppet plays for his nieces, then simple stage plays and poems. He joined a New Orleans writers' critique group, and began learning in earnest, finding out how awful his first efforts were.

During his college years and right after while working for Chevron, he wrote many of the fun songs you see here. He also wrote some poetry, and love poems for his fiancée.

He continued writing songs on occasion, but became interested in script writing for stage plays. Those are included in another anthology.

The poems and songs in this volume were saved and assembled for the first time in 2022. They span the spectrum of love poems, sad songs, ditties and jingles, songs about faith and God, silly songs, fun songs (as my children call them). Julie, our youngest, was lucky enough to have several birthday songs written for her, and sung at the restaurant for all the other patrons to enjoy.

If ever you meet my children, ask them to sing you the "Fun Song" song.

As "*lagniappe*" (or bonus), I've included six short pieces including a puppet play.

John has been married to Phyllis for 43 years, and together they have raised three children, and now have six grandchildren. They live in Lafayette, Louisiana.

www.ingramcontent.com/pod-product-compliance
Lightning Source LLC
LaVergne TN
LVHW090531110826
845146LV00003B/1053

* 9 7 9 8 9 8 5 7 0 3 9 3 1 *